For Family & Friends

Living & Dead

CONTENTS

The life that produces writing can't be written about. It is a life carried on without the knowledge even of the writer, below the mind's business and noise, in deep unlit shafts where phantom messengers struggle toward us, killing one another along the way; and when a few survivors break through to our attention they are received as blandly as waiters bringing more coffee.

— Tobias Wolff, *Old School*

Birth Order

Each of you the same since birth.

The first, early, refusing to share this world.
Breached. When forced to present,
quiet and determined.
You did as we pleased.

The second, timely, full force shoulders breaking
mother from end to bloody end,
twisted and threatened,
rapidly rushing from the protected
quiet to a cold steel operating room.

Baby, giving false impressions, fooling those
who know better, then falling without effort
into nurses hands. Running from parking lot
to delivery. So fast the blood came in buckets.

Always, the father is pushed away, useless to the bodily
business of the world. Yes, you all remain the same,
your birth has shaped you.
Quiet and determined.
Forceful and in the way.
Quick and easy
to make others sacrifice.

In my science experiment, I will ask
every mother how her child entered this new space.
Then, I would understand the man
as he emerged before himself.
Still, I would never ask after my birth.
Would it be human to possess
the fragile knowledge of that sweet fruit?

Molly

Tiny motor mouthed brat
sleeping like a freckled angel,
bikini-clad, I write to you
from familiar barren ground.

It's June, the most distracted
month. You wake pouting
for want of a cold cup holder
and a candy necklace.

I see you now, after absence
and through marital history,
your face fuller, taller too.
You tell me to devote myself

to a life of patience to you
while you stare into the simple
yellow light of a mirror white
floor, judging my degeneration.

My life watches as you go.
Trying to save your expressions of
our remembering.

The Elfette

The elfette suggests, "I know
what she wants, something practical."
Hearing her this year only for
reasons you know, you listen and
lo, behold, the elfette is not just
inspirational but right. The stars
aligned, the mall avoided, presents
emerge, materialize between
the fast-food health shop and
the used athletic equipment store.
What do they mean?

Separate and apart, a zen sand garden,
for miniature peace. A chime bell for
harmonious dinner calls, bathroom cream,
lotions and oils, for self-luxuriousness,
pampered, a subtle beauty. The grand finale,
the origin of the treasure hunt. The baby blue
all purpose, you have one too,
keychain tool kit, scissors included.

Practical, prepared, and equal.
Life is good. Wear and remember.
Pretend. Appearances are our need.
"Stay, happy birthday," as the elfette's eyes smile.

Bukowski Misses the Funeral

At sundown
we bury her bird.
Escape the cage
fragile flyer and learn
it's a dog eat bird world.
The ceremony performed
rapidly, in the Jewish way,
words said, warnings
for a future service.
Brother sends his regrets,
he could not stand to bury
another bird. Life is tragic.

We bury the bird in the hole
left from last summer's boredom.
Behind the wall, the dog cannot jump
to dig up her prey.
Finish the work now,
you have purpose.
The shovel can turn its last,
flattening the tomb to earth.

Placing the stone I think of you
in Los Angeles, drinking, cursing,
whoring. You write of men's dreams,
poker, the fights, the racetrack.
Not for you this domestic
bliss, gone to the next woman,
big breasted, peroxide and drunk.
It only matters to you that you live your life.
Too bad, really, you always miss the
child's tears at the funeral.

Good Dad

It's a good Dad who makes conversation
with his son at the dinner table, asking
what he bought his girlfriend for her
birthday, knowing full well the answer
and knowing the son has no compunction
to declare before mother and little sister
and God, "Handcuffs."

Mother's face in disgust gives chance
for bright sister to ask "What?" and before
the good Dad can determine steel or
velvet, the happy child suggests brother
buy his girl a thong.

Rehabilitation is the aging parents' hobby
of pain. "You mean shoes, or do you want
to start at the girls school tomorrow?"
Giggles and squirms and lilting retort,
"Boys like see through."

To explain to this aspiring siren,
daughter, that she does not want to know
life in ways men/boys like her brother
consider, and after all, she has
lived with him and witnessed his beer
guzzling, cigar smoking, bored dazed eyes.

Good Dad then retreats, rebuked
to the childless den of his maturity.
Leave the girls to the women-folk
goes the old saw, from a culture
once known, betrayed by experience.
Be the keeper of secrets, beguiled
by life's charismatic ennui,
not the honest broker, bargaining
to see the stuff of others souls.

Twenty-One Year Old Boy Poet

Just when you thought
you had grown to be a man,
twenty-one year old boy
poet, howling on Bourbon Street,
the genetic pattern, unknown,
shows its haunted face to you.

Kicked by love,
the muse returns,
destiny is renewed.
Your muse shadowed
by betrayal, young poet,
commands, we are not
what we appear.

Enter under the Magdalena
kneeling, crossing, purification
by narrative. Follow these
same souls to the street where you
have known them, yes familiar,
but not church.

Another deception, the speaker,
urbane and genteel, enters the day
where survival must be won.
Is this the same soul? The clown cries,
the undertaker smiles. Before you surge
confidence, remember your love masks
your innocence. It may be too late.

We are granted glimpses,
moments of beauty,
familiarity healing the soul.
Then forgotten, wind across the sand.
Write this, boy poet. You
born blessed can not guess
the clues of your fate
known in the end only by others.

53

After the most elegant champagne on the menu toast,
before the traditional rendering song, the birthday
boy takes life's meter. Never a dispassionate
observer, he remembers older celebrations, peers
into the silent disintegration of his mother's eyes.
Burning moments from sun's dawn, he is older now,
and replaces ambition's frustrations with love's loss.
Hearing hearts beat melancholy across a tender breast,
he knows the smallest act is mystery. Time
restarts itself. The boy smiles. Grief is still
prospective. There is evening enough to misdirect
demons, let joy behold the minds of friends, lovers,
mentors. Calculating that this is no less than all that is,
accounted for at last. Changing attachments, pretending
a talent for indifference, he vows this year to heighten
his mind's labor. Order the tiramisu, one candle please.

Grandma

Watching last possessions leaving through the back door
she smiles at the fifty years' static rising from the oriental
rugs she prized. Investments against a market she could
not control nor give her concern. Eyes still bright, gleaming
wit and rage at ninety-nine, she does not notice the mothball
smell preserving the flowered silk purse, the square
heeled shoes. Almost fashionable.

The rolling metal chair she calls home has replaced
the painted English upholstery from which she shared holidays
celebrating the miracle of Oz turning green from the old
black and white console. Football championships covered
in snow brought by the wonder of electricity and ritual
meals served with dull regularity to distant relatives glowing
in the warmth of winter's invited sixty degrees.

Struggling to gift her life's collections she uncovers
memories of weekends at the drive-in, already a grandmother
these forty five years past, concealing the drunk second
husband in the garage of her faith. Happiness, experienced
long ago, now balances empty on sorrow's edge, exhausting
the clarity of age.

Watching generations of her men move cherry wood
and ivory to a neighborhood forbidden to her youth, she
strives to connect this ghost world, hapless and
precarious to the old ballroom of her confusion
of a wedding, dresses, boulevards, and sisters
devoured by time.

Ignoring the silence beyond tomorrow she grapples
with the Doctor's cold pronouncement, neither cruel
nor suspenseful, unforgiving in her returned stare of truth
that will withstand the last pain. Her long elderly face,
hair thinning, will not be dazzled by his poor human
vision slipped through the depths. She knows she can
not win the eternal bet.

Struggling against the decrepitude of the empty room
before her reign, left to solitary escapes, her timed
thoughts verge on the task of living day to day.
Knowing so long as an acerbic tongue can defend
against natures incursions, she remains in the exile
of a life gathered and lost. She has had no more or
less than others. She will determine when it is
time to go.

Childhood's Den

Waking into excited night I seek comfort in the monthly
magazines, an overstuffed chair. Staring into faces grown
old I wonder what will be disclosed. The bookshelves,
ceiling high in the dark are steadied by the hard backed
Modern Library collected as a shield against time. Framed
by the window of their extinction a wooden stand supports
an American dictionary opened eternally to Marquise.
Impressionist print and Flemish medieval woodcut found
at a flea market sale serve as a European museum for young
eyes. How enticing this comfortable room created to pay
our bills and balance every Saturday. Home is our sacred
space, eaves protecting against the coming summer storm.
Adobe wall, shoulder high, divides us from our neighbors'
mysteries. Here is born all adventure my small heart needs,
palming, catching, aiming imagined spheres across a small corner
and scribbling the first aspirations of my fictional life.

Advice to an Old Man

Before he leaves we will walk together.
His color fades as habit drives our vain debate.
My scornful words will heed his hardened wisdom.
His gathered will reduced by force of age,
I counsel motion, it cannot be buried. He sweeps
under life's stubborn proof, knowing as long
as we are here we can stir the stuff of eternity,
smiling at the unwatered rose of time.

How I Missed My High School Reunion

I live among ghosts.
The streets I drive are empty.
Dead or gone, or worse.
Do not compel me,
guilty one, to visit these specters
in the flesh. Girls with skin
pure as their thoughts forbidden,
now, turned to cellulite, wrinkled
and desirous of youth
in platinum and paint.
Boys, full of laughter,
adventure, now filled with gout,
remembering pleasures fueled
by alcohol and cocaine. My ghosts
come, winsome,
craving friendship and love. Bloated
faces carved from tiresome jobs,
children, divorce, fortunes made and lost,
still dream of cherry filled bowls out of hands'
grasp. Life is not confirmed in chronological
meter. Instead I remember those
who have escaped reunion, the ignored, the despised,
souls driven home by family unseen.
Raise a hand to the quiet, the lost, the cowardly.
In your laughing glib comfort tell of your sleepless
nights, your secrets of self-destruction, the stories
that reveal your missing circle of protection.
Tonight, go ahead, proclaim all of this, we are here,
your long lost childhood friends.

Colors

How is the wine and book and women's
stock club transformed tonight? What
possesses you to disguise your desires, to
collapse our natural divisions? Is it too
much for me to hide in the study, watching
television, watching the eternal season
of sport? With pretzels and beer I am whole.
Do I need to understand the matrix of my neighbor's
personality? Isn't it enough if I think he is a nice
guy, she a tempestuous ditzy eyed siren? Their
needs and struggles, values and stresses are enough
for them. As you mouth secrets under compelled
oath, do not take my tight silence as arrogance
or fear. What I know is that your soft orange heart
can not bear the gold truth made blue by the fact
of our long green experience.

Poets Meet at the Racetrack

It had been years. I was glad you recognized
me, graying and in folds Funny how the mind
consistently conjures. Can you believe there is
more to this world if you stay in place? I thought
of you when I walked through the gate.
Who else do I know who has written
artfully of this place. Finally, we exchanged
old recognition, connected.

Trading seats at the counter you walk
me to the viewing circle, scoffing at my zany
intuition. We repeat at leisure our children's tales,
re-telling misdeeds. Wives by our sides open
separate doors with staccato syntax, grimace at
our chosen banalities. The bell sounds and we rush
to watch the destructive stimulations, wretched
today, vividly joyous in sun drenched memory.

Edged at the tape we wonder how to mix our posed
austerity with greed. We walk through program filled
aisles, garbage flipped into the bins of tomorrow.
You, the battered chronicler must stay and watch
the sad story of your pony playing companion,
hoping to take home and remember one new detail,
one complete vignette.

Remembering Broken Vows

If you are not the luckiest man alive, then please explain
the sunshine lighting your canopied home,
the cottonwood shadowing the canyon wall
where we overlook the grass and clay.
No one could understand your young arrogance,
your stubborn principal. You got what you wanted.

Cello and violin conjure a vision of veiled beauty uncovered
by ritual dance and too much wine. The contract
of devotion is sealed in broken glass. Metal rings are
exchanged to remember the core of your honor. Families
mend for a moment, forgetting their anger, their loss of each other.

In tears brief smiles displayed on this appointed night
wet lace and friendship. Alone now, your heart is opened
by remembered vows, hearkening to that joyful day long
lost to humorless bitter quibble.

After the Miss

At dusk he walked from the pot-holed
asphalt neighborhood turning broad
back a last time on the bent rims, hanging
chain metal nets that ground his failed
attempt. Arcing from his hand like
a cautionary prayer the empty bleachers
do not applaud.

Everybody wants the last shot,
the bawdy occasion before worshipful
eavesdroppers who ignore
the attractions confronting
tomorrow's lament. Roguish quarry
never distinguishes between love and grief,
unconsciousness and death, until it is too late.

In solitude he unravels the lies
obscured in the cold repetitions
of leather pounding wood, shooting
daybreak lay-ups to forget the sober
dalliance of lost affections. He listens
to the gossip of merchants confined
to checking decorated signatures

and wishes for days spying through
fences and doll house windows, when
racing legs brought warmth and passing
smiles that never knew the possibility
of irretrievable motion or lifetime regret.

Wendy, Hook & Pan

Lost boy,
tender, cruel,
demon of disguise.
Touching something feminine
like the great pirates who
have given up hope,
never humor. Heartless child
caring for no one but himself
flaunts with curling lip
a sacred truth lost
in deaf December.
Resolution exhausted in his
combustible soul
forever burning dreams.

Old man,
in black and steel,
sighing under his crushed
outsider's cool that watches
the light lick the edges
of dawn. His searing reserve,
what remains of an ever receding
faith. Losing one's place is negligible.
Sustained by an ancient knowledge,
we are still here.
Savvy old patron, ventriloquist,
self satisfied and despised, he glimpses
the ransacked remains of a heart
crying too late.

Homebound and protected
the flawed guardian of memory
yearns for men long gone.
In closed spaces she searches dry text
for a fervor that does not fade.

Renewed in time remaining
her repose precedes performance
on demand. Naiveté is revealed
as the chill of common turbulence,
wanting only the surprise of sensuality
to light her quiet smile. Her honeymoon
luggage lies in the middle distance.
This silent woman listens under bedclothes
for fairies — and rogues.

Wedding in Black and White

The blue Victorian looms over sedans
filled with celebrants pretending loyalties
loathsome and sad. Inside, the one armed
minister will attempt, with words alone,
to perform a miracle — bonding spirits
through obstacles of identity,
layers of stereotype and expectation.
The smiling bride and the cool groom
ignore their tensions internalized
through repressive convention. Laughing at
chastisement, they jump the broom,
coming of age in a rapture soon belied by earthly
abandonment. Under the wine cellar
door the mother whispers her secrets to no one.
Older, wiser, she prays her daughter's restless
agitation rebukes the nuance and
ambiguity of every human moment. A train
whistle signals the return down the aisled street
laced with marigold and orange. The father,
trailing, almost cries at the decline of this double
consciousness, shunning filial loyalty at the
pinnacle of complexity indistinguishable
from his heart's transfiguring fire. The best
man smiles, large and brave, remembering the
bride's attractive resistance the night before. Her
palpable impulse against his chest, confirming shared
knowledge. On shifting ground the guests share
dance floor and cake restrained in their reveling by
a poverty of spirit, time prancing and stealing
children's memories, gloried at dawn.

Reunion

Early January sunset, we listen
to stories told by friends away
from time's aging. The less hardy
ones did not survive, and we
wonder why. We smile at our
craft, remember together days
of adrenaline, exhaustion, secret
meetings in the shadow of the
cathedral. The good will there,
funded by a government now lost
to fear and self-serving. This kin
celebrates the hope of return,
to meet again in twenty years,
looking still unravaged by time,
flaunting our ideals, remembering
wayward travels, days spent playing
barroom games charged to a distant
payer, justified in being the good
bad guys. We remember the jailed,
who bear the mark of society gone
wrong – the bad check writers, drug
abusers, poor and dumb, and those
for whom a four by eight steel cell
provides a safe rest. In this
cauldron, we forced the working hours
to distill a humanity we drank
when liberty allowed
our will to work. We thought
life was simple and would endure
forever in boisterous jest. In
fading light we trumpet our presence,
while time's disappointment remains
hidden in unproclaimed memories.

The Hollow Man

The hollow man came home today.
Smiling as if the years had not stripped
his soul bare. We exchange small talk.
Do you still believe in the miracle of cure?

Led to his private room
the prodigal confronts his fate.
Slowly, then instantaneously, his eyes bloat
shut. The mask dissolves and he feels
what he expects others might want to hear.
He mimics echoes manipulated by
a shadow past. Wanting a gut full of shared
emotion, he chases poison.

Forced now to say good-bye to the last
connection, to a world aspired, and falsely
claimed, we hug and grip to disguise the bleak
walls of return. The hobbling, freshly
shocked street woman blocks his path.
She smiles, here there is no harm in courtesy.

He passes and she whispers, "Good
riddance to bad rubbish."

Ode to Billy Collins

Imagine the scorn on the faces of those who read
the American poet laureate, only to find his genius
is doing nothing to disguise his identity as the non-descript
fellow at the mall, buying the discount suit or wishing
for the Caribbean vacation. A middle aged balding white
man of diminished build, in tweed, mistaken for the certified
public accountant you let go at the office. Sure, there is
a pretension of jazz in the background and a flavor of eastern
religion displayed as curiosity, but really no more than any
of us find on the national public radio or the spiritual shelves
at the big box bookstore. So, it is common comfort and
a disturbing turn in our familiarity of what he is. Wouldn't
we like to believe that art is something different than
ourselves? We are not so different from our aspiration.
If we observe, in time, our ordinary abstractions, we wake
to the present moment and record the existing self.

~ ❁ ~

Cricket

Cricket
out of season,
cold cryer
through the sealed
window.

Without friend.
No one bothers
her noise.

Autumn Morn

Old man's smile
Fall breeze
House of brick
Morning run.

Unexpected beauty
Makes a place
Of rest,
If not escape.

Touching Grace

In a late spring moment of desert dawn,
naked, the walled garden protecting
our flesh, alert to the cool pink
light brightening color and definition,
we touch grace. Peacefully holding
hands, the glaring long day looms.
Inevitability is delayed within our construct
of time occupied by morning
scent of creosote and moon's last fall.

Foothills Ladies Discover Nirvana at the Gym

Three fat women
run slowly
on grey treadmills.

Burn calories daily
exchange repetitions
of aspiring children,
wayward husbands and
work.

Smile knowingly,
lives controlled, scheduled
and reduced to seven
square miles. Music
lessons, softball, fondling
fruits for the sweetest pulp.

The sweat hour ends
in the parking lot
moist with dusk, illuminated
by the full moon balanced
on the eastern range.

I walk behind, surprised
by knowing their lives are poetry,
traveling into a rarely
noticed night.

Urban Converts Announce their Return

Before day breaks the only thought of value
is presented in the cookie cutter rubber
franchised cool coffee house. The balding
grey trimmed bifocal man is handed warm
brew and the New York Times by the girl
behind the counter. Both are of faith lost.
Was it the insincere teacher, rock and roll,
the tiresome world seen whole? Was the fable
swallowed completely, without context, the first
cause? Regardless, they can hardly hide who
they are, recognized by common blood and energy,
drawn visible in time of danger and pride.

They grimace in silence, they know their origins,
acknowledge the old neighborhood, comfortable and alone.
Declare, as the change passes that they
will not forget each other. The eyes' light delivers
them to awareness.
The steps at the door of return
are not steep. An image, a melody, a human touch
can show them home. There is no shame in return.
The choice is made by the forgotten ones
announcing
we are all carried away
by someone else
from this world.

The Bartender's Regret

Four grey men
blanched by time
seek life from
the same well.

Stiff with regret
from faded
pasts, haunted by
forbidden shadows.

One lives by will
and prayer, no earthly
presence bleak enough
to staunch his yellow smile.

Another turns on the
void, demanding
always to take the
other path.

A third seeks the
unknown, touched by
the warm hand of
a brother lost to sorrow.

The fourth, blood
indignant to the power of
unseen necessity. Gone,
without regret.

I am the fifth. Left asking,
Did I keep myself
too much to myself,
denied the fellowship of a
common moment?

Sanctuary Prayer

This is the place where I am comfortable,
where the world can not take my essence.
The window provides sun when I want it.
I am surrounded by books, remnants of
others' pasts. I need not reach far
for what will sustain me. This is my center.

To extend is to risk. From my perch, my cave,
my hollow, I strengthen my heart and choose
to pray. The waters are said to bring spirits
of courage and righteousness, I have enough
in the inhalation of their vapors that tell me
stay the course.

When I wander I lose my compass. In my seat,
carpeted by art and dreams, memory
provides impenetrable peace. Custom does
not sadden my tired eyes. What is meant
to be will overcome our human weakness or
otherwise.

Direct us from acquisition at our center. Instead,
study the ballerinas in the wheat fields, the delicate
script disclosed in dim light, the piano medley
in the deserted street. Sleep at morning's last star,
guided by quicksilver, let other pulses quicken at the
light of day.

Taxi Driver Dreams

I have turned off the television.
I have turned off the radio.
The news is what I see
and what I do not see.
I listen for what is real
and eternal. It is quiet —
as quiet as the creation;
as quiet as it will be at
the boundaries of infinity.

Touching peace the world
returns. Tires hum, doors
slam, voices call, newspapers
hit the pavement. If only I
could bottle sea air for the August
desert or inoculate tranquility
into the veins of my worldly passage.

Turning, my vision slows and a
coughing woman splays across
my backseat, sharing fare to
our common home.

Jewel Box

What riches of the earth are hidden in this sealed heart?
Found under the floor, beneath a spirit in fetal position
the jewel box holds an imperfect world abandoned
in mystery, stimulated by confusion.

The secret panel lost within the beveled door reveals
dancers unvarying in their grace, robust warm sweat
glowing from the truth of thin skins sealing budding
flowers of beauty that vanish with the passing night.

Pierced to the heart, this world packs small suitcases
filled with old loves staring at private forgotten wrongs.
Unmoored by detail they remember our daunting modesty
over vodka martinis, willing history to be altered by alluring

acts without consequence. The box knows there is no such
creation. Returning further inward the magic world fills with
words angered by adrenaline, deformed by hands that sweep
us away into straddling shocks of calamity and violence.

Imagine random intersections of love caressing your belly
to satisfying fullness. The box recedes through mirrors to
an inner sanctum without numbers, time, or currency. There is
no score. Happiness is found in the sweetness of stolen glances

echoing the musicians feel for a rhythm that matters.
The leaves disclose another lost October. Tears dry
yellow and red in the portal to the right. Taking needle and ink
the holder of the box asks you to inscribe some eternal wisdom.

Slow the valley of time, bathe in the fomenting distance, there are
boundaries we never cross.

Neighborhood Bhudda

Speaking simple words, ornate wisdom
I walk like the neighborhood Bhudda.
Visiting the dry cleaner, the thin blonde,
bleached in hair and pallor, smiles crookedly as
she receives my laundry's secrets, my need
for ritual cleaning. Why is the lesson never learned?
Our exchange signifies more than history
wrought by senators and generals.
When she chooses to listen.

I tread to the next task, opening
the hardware store, a mystery of latches, wires,
screws and metals folded into aisles, requiring another
education. My words curiously stored are useless here.
The chores end with a tribute to the sky —
blue, clear, cloudless and accepting. Tea and egg salad
await my travel into afternoon nap, slowly fading
as the week ends in peace.

～ ❀ ～

Feeding the Homeless

Rushing from glass, steel, and paper
to the littered auditorium, the schoolhouse
clock sounds the minutes to make coffee,
fill the salt and pepper, find juice, milk and
crackers. Pre-school parents walk oblivious
to the social nuisance graciously hosted.
Adjusting the antennae on the aging television
to find local news at six, chicken in the
oven, rice on the stove. The homeless trudge
in. Bring me your tired, your poor, your despised.
Weather reports sleet and wind as the women
and children drag their cots and blankets to the
nearest room heater. The gloves and socks,
oranges and bananas, shampoo and soap, are
gone before dinner is served.

Quiet smiles, appreciation, thanksgiving for
a small favor. Time for chocolate cake before
the smoke in the lot. Clouds descend, the
door closed to the wind. Blues Brothers,
paperbacks and street talk sounds in
the crowded room as the frail wheeze to sleep.
Only the young continue in a video stare.
I turn out the hall light. I walk into the streetlight
night. My soul is cleansed to receive tomorrow's
metered grime.

My Dogs Vote for President

The body too long rested,
now tired, like a shadow
wall image that sparks
the adrenaline of thought,
the assessing glint of
the grey haired clerk recommending
popular paperbacks and smiling
at random connections inverted
reminds me of parallel worlds,
a double vision. The first,
ideologically bankrupt, the second,
where character is collected.

Disdainful of threats imposed
by pre-emptive zealotry, he
witnesses empires collapsing
and cheers. A born again patrician,
unbound by nationalism and
unrestrained double speak, he leads
those without history into the world
of not.

A predator in Brooks Brothers suit
courting rich merchants of celebrity
he sings to the imperious arrogance
of occupation, excusing atrocity with
God's will, never doubting his apocalyptic
vision of war, beyond victory or loss,
dissimilating a gay condemnation
of what he does not know.

Our cities lie shamed and polarized,
riddled by the travels and speeches
of cowards and liars, dictators with
invisible arms, without intuitive honor.
One page of condemnation will not
eliminate the ills of this macabre show.

There is no leash law
in the neighborhood dog world
of my imagination. Howling
through washes, gathering night
adventure, snouts in trash cans
dodging the walls of
chlorinated human pleasure.
My mind races through yards
bound by the thoroughfares
of shocking death. The moon
lights our half seen acre,
language shared in barks
and whimpers, like boyhood
friends, breaking curfew.
Poetry rings true our return.
Sleeping days and escaping
to a burrowed world where
covered and protected our
senses snuggle and are satisfied
by smell. Clove, markings,
the bitches scent, touching,
without regret, the whole divine.

Remembering Shared Atrocity

Fatal conflict remembered in black
and white transformed by a perverse
delirium to digital color and real time.
A wilderness interrogation ends
with pistol at soldier's head. Death slips into
the nightly drone with shared euphemisms.
Next, the maelstrom of bondage, naked,
cries in agony, flees on a dirt road
pursued by napalm fire.
Driven by a culture no longer cared for,
complicit and debased by war, we await the
buoyant transformation from the
next pornographic camera, shot by the perpetually
incredulous, pure of heart. Gathered by
voyeurs contracting amnesia of the long distance
mayhem we are shadowed by a cloud
unleashed by those who write bold history,
gradually disclosed as superficial and atrocious.
Living in a virtual reality of bombs
clicked and pointed on screens
no different from those found on laser
discs at the bottom of the neighborhood
market bin. Dulled and jaded by images
of images, we succumb to an invitation
to entertainment motivated by unquestioned profit. Sweat
stained skulls, gathered in exotic places and never
recognized as our own, discovered as we
release new skepticism that does not hinder our
nightly prayers.

Independence Day

If I was born of different station —
military brass, for instance, or poetic
aristocracy, a damaged star conscience
forged in a private jail,

I might have ridden in the Independence
Parade, flirting with the old flamingos
translucent pink under grey, disrupting
households with my banal words,
rattling trifles,

Or stood with democracy's fathers,
old and wigged and distinct
from the buried will. A single objector,
my shrunken heart simplified by wild
wayward prophets.

The island's distinct spell
makes me articulate. A lantern
moving wobbly debris home.

Eyeing forbidden scrawl,
my voice aches for road's end.
Towering tempers shape apology.
A lost girl calls game's ruin.

Here, my other life witnesses as
the unnecessary show of force
claims another innocent without
remark. Life's isolation meets terror.
A doctor's impatience asks relief.

I hold, as they run. My anarchic
hollowness fixes union and rebounds.
Yes, if I had been someone else,
linear, patriotic, I might have felt
a treasured cell of pitiful joy.

Sunday Morning Poet

If I were searching for tradition
at the turn of this new century,
I would walk to the end
of my driveway on Sunday morning,
in my underwear and sandals,
wincing at the chill in winter,
or feeling for a still breeze
in spring. Stretching my calves
up the hill to my doorpost
I would tell those looking
for clues to our post-modern
commonality to observe me
sitting at kitchen table,
drinking coffee, eating rye
toast, lightly buttered, listening
to public radio or folk or
jazz or pre-game talk.
Multi-tasking through ears
never closed and eyes not
wanting to open, I would look
up at my examiner and point
to my absorption of book
reviews, editorials and the
gossip scandal news. Declaring
"Do not seek truth in
history and public documents. This
is who we are. This is all you
need to know."

Tax Dollars

My lifetime contribution to this great country
now is spent in bombs dropped on foreign soil.
I remain as calm as any German citizen in 1939,
going about my business, my daily tasks, ignoring
the papers, the radio. If I do not know the detail
I am not implicated. No one asked me,
and if they had, no one would have listened.

Why They Do It

Eyes white.
Not why you think they do it.

The breakfast explosion thrill.
No.

The smoking windows stench,
targeting devastation burned
through metal, flesh charred.
Touch.

To witness market luxuries
incinerated before occupiers
now uncertain in the shimmer
of disillusionment.
Closer.

Organization men.
Celebrating eviction's ecstasy
Acting out the suicide's secret.
A hero's revenge for the comrade
ravaged, a soldier's love, hopeless,
Obsessed.

The campaign outs
aggravated invaders
savaged by dislocated
martyrs rootless and scorned.
Casting prophetic dignity
at the discontent faithful, prepared
to butcher the unnerved,
splintered by restlessness.
Fascination.

For them, death finds the moment
worldly withdrawal.

New Orleans

Barges flow over the city.
The river carries the port
to Slidell. Down Claiborne
vessels shake, resurrect
the poor, unwashed each
holding his own ticket to fear.

Inundated, nowhere to go,
exposed as the cargo of dollars
wallows in smug rhetoric,
and sinks the black menace,
the crippled, the huddled.

As homes drown in lunar sunsets,
aging mannequins and neon
infants appear from nowhere,
astonished at the ignorance
and neglect revealed
in the drying flood.

High Wire Walker

In not such a far away time
nimble gawkers filled with
ghastly curiosity stared into
the void.

From a cathedral hideaway
the black clad performer
stands, eyes riveted on a
meticulous balance.

Haunted by magical dances
he punctuates the moon
with a high wire salute.

The drizzly morning, otherwise
suited only for feeding pigeons,
is background. He breaks locks in stone
hallways, sneaks metal cords
across a depth of dreams.

Exposed, the rolling wind
howls through his gray hair, daredevil
to a far horizon he holds thin air,
consumed by sorrow.

His glorious youthful stunt,
a premonition of collapse,
materializes at altitude. His skinny
belly, like springing cable, walks on.
The vertical concrete playgrounds
of his imagination forever crash
to dust. What once captured
eccentric space is gone.

Coming of Age in Brooklyn

The last time I was accused
of ignoring the relatives, sullen,
I slammed my sister's door.
Her talking and chewing of fish bones
filleted her child's throat. My
formative pain grew cold with
the infuriated discipline of elders'
frustration. Strokes of feared
concern soothed the heartbreak
forever blazed across my growing
rage. Run into the street, the old
proximity crying for neighbors, tailors,
doctors, hawkers.

Midnight summoned another slamming door,
not mine, hiding the echoing memories
of a truth I could not know.
A golden cocoon preserved my courage.
Unconsciously I walked the concrete
streets, a once-a-week intimacy
at the corner grocery where the world news
increased the unsteadiness in the faces I
accompanied.

Between holidays my horizons grew,
my anger avenged by the momentarily
forgotten losses of Saturday
mornings dedicated to eternal sadness.
Had I known happiness, that unnatural
state, must retreat as life takes its ordinary toll,
I could have forgotten my history in
routine not saved by the street or school or lost
dark joy. The corner is turned. New roads
are found. I am returned to the interior of my making.

Fragment

Summer never stirs in the Black Forest.
There, the chocolate milking goddess
plays through the white eternity of winter,
wanting her lover's shadow to take her as
he whispers into her adoring breast.

First Love

This is for all my loves
and near loves
running
in night light,
extracting spare meaning
out of unions with memory.

No regrets from love created
in cigar smoke and
bourbon drunk to life
altering distortion,
bring focus
on what I am and was.

Time's dangerous longings
caused us to shake hands
in reconciliation
with our melancholy.
Like drunks on a lamp post
we gave each other
something to lean on.

In goodness we misspent
our wonder at the wall
of enduring illusion.
I remember. Do you
remember now that I am gone?

As a youth I buried the wind,
constructed passion
while bathing and binding us
in our bed of love's folly.
You dislodged gravity behind my back
in midnight drinking bouts that numbed
my guard room ignorance. Merchant
of laughter, you tried to hold
immortality in a perilous heart
broken by summer rain.

Ours was a rented world, perfect in solitude.
Now, I see you holding your leather books,
sipping pink vodka and dreaming of yard
sale treasures won with irregular satire.

Can you understand
our friendship, unseen in the loose
buttons and charged remarks
fashioned by a touch barely
known at all.

So you, gone forever, and I
will be quiet in loneliness.
Peering from the porch over bare
feet, containing emotion and
self-love beneath fallen mesquite.

Those who are nimble in love do not
need more. Your parting words told
me, "Eat the crust." I already knew
this was the best I was going to get.

Afternoon Handyman

Afternoon handyman, not the first suspicion, what harm
in unperceived dalliance. Gifted to perform manual
tasks, plumbing and tuning, beneath me, where was your
time. We partnered, but left incomplete she found a hole
in space. Now gone, no longer kept to give human service,
no longer collecting metals and tools. No rummaging in
half empty homes for dire treasures presented as pure
pleasure. In loving forbearance you kept me in conversation,
helpless, without wit, what other ignorance could blind me
to silks left strewn over leather. The newspaper announces
there will be no resurrection, your special fix. Surviving
on necessity's blind eye to the obvious, you found lost
emotions stunted in suburban hills. Disease slowed but did
not withhold your internal freedom. One leaves, another
pines. The third makes tribute to piety soiled. Lovers cry
alone under roofs recast with handprints, shadowed by a heart
treacherous as the solitary image stumbling at dawn
driven to human separateness. Where did you think we all
end? The rattle in the clock signaled the skirmish that hides
inevitable fear. She was no diva but you made her sing.
She is left alone and dimly lit on a shallow stage looking for
repair in a puddle of chips and ashes.

Maturing Love

When I left you to your own devices
at happy hour, for a wooden desk,
dimly lit, it was an acknowledgment.
Like the half-time at the high school
basketball game where I held a soft
hand that did not respond, ever again.

Or, after the night on the rocks in front
of her parents' home, her father called,
telling mine I was not to see her young
lips again, I was too old. Not understanding
at sixteen, after all, she was months
younger, well, maybe, a year.
Still, the same, notice
that what we had was done.

This leaving then, not a public declaration
or a noticed separation, just a line drawn,
one we felt covering our souls, telling us,
the next time you hear the pitted sound
on wooden steps, you will not be waiting
in gladness but dread. We can hope the
echo will go on or disappear, agree that
until eternity we have better things to do
than each other, or agree to be friends, siblings,
lovers, or agree to a sadder maturity for
appearance sake.

The Word

Begin with
a word,
the word,
the right word.

My mind dances,
captures a shadow
escapes a midnight fire.
Passion and illusion
illuminate the window
I open to spy
on false piety
that comforts
the distortion of our captivity.

Vibrant island, move
souls who shun community.
I pray for breath, taunt
sleep, torment the tongue
and pen to put it right. Why
are love and loyalty lost
in the reign of our pride?

The Last Supper

Good. One half hour of solitude
to say good-bye. I have tried
to re-invent the world. I cannot.
Our meal together leaves a hunger
for shared nourishments we cannot
forget. No longer shall we
create delicacies at knifepoint.
The sugared peaches, erotic in
blackened pans, boil heated relations,
savory with cream and blood
left to dry and curdle.
Others can wonder at our coupled
mysteries. Draped in white, the
kitchen was your altar, food the religion
of a childhood burdened by history
and hunger. My champagne
and chocolate were never enough.
What remains is the blood orange taste
haunted by a family wistful for
the aromas of joy, love, life.
We prepared our table with mindless
discipline, turning from the wanton
appetites lying within. What food
could satisfy? Our dessert heralded
the great distance at ritual's end.
Now, finding you wrapped
and sparkling with the other,
I remember banquets and
street snacks, precious tastes thirty years
past. As the chicory is served, the spotted
remains on the wedding china are familiar
with melancholy and shame.
At day's end the pantry door closes
behind dirty basement steps, a cracked door
hurries the forbidden treat. There are no
more fires. With each bite
we remember, oyster garnished with rosemary.
Be comfortable in the marble chair, we will
not share a meal again.

Calling the Rockpile

When the call comes to the speeding sedan
it is not as if your voice shows any sign of life.
I am directed to that small place where I
conceal myself and am whole. I climb the
winding hill and inflict pleasure that fragments
the day. At the crossroad I stare into the distance
where I see my fate. My heart tangled in
spider tendrils, grows through a rockpile of ruins
we call love. Only when I leave, momentarily
pleased, do the long hours of empty thought begin
the slow disintegration of my half content bemusement.

Rancho de la Osa

Returning to the remains of his labor
ravaged by time the wearied old one
gives blessing and smiles for what he
knew. New paint arrives, purple, lavender,
navy blue. The iron polished, the rotted
boards removed, good history found.
The diplomats memorabilia pressed
and framed, Navajo rugs dusted in cellar
mud unboxed to hang with modern art.

This haunt will not be forgotten, even the
aging caretaker, without energy to mend,
is sent to cemetery with honor. Heirs jealous
of illiquid love are banished and for bargain
sold. The land endures. Here is your chance
to create time, balance the mesquite, grade
paths and gate the drive. The founders watch
from afar. Make refuge for bird, bear, big cat,
deer and thirst starved traveler.

Language laughed away must serve.
Build again and rest. The work is good.

After Love

Age does not dampen or inflame desire.
The enamored stomach flattens at the
thought of outstretched limbs,
youth's artful visions. Eyes close.
Unspoken dreams of shyness rest on
celluloid without imagination.
When the mobile rings without echo a familiar
depression and hunger enter your unwalled
garden. There is only vision. Blue
mountains touched by sunlit snow melting
into the perennial stream is my ecstasy now.

Insomnia

Those nights when my checkerboard sleep
is disturbed by an adrenaline drip, racing
me past late night television, the weekly
novel and the B.B.C., I walk across the city
park guided by a single lamp, disregarding
fear. Imagining shattered lives taking refuge
in the cool distance of the swing set, I construct
the morning challenge in the shallows of sleep
swayed depression. The ball field invites
my funneled energy to run the short bases.
My maze of purpose is relinquished in the mockery
of inconsequence. At home plate I walk into a
slow somnolence, the shadows hinting at yesterday's
chance acquaintances, deluded clowns navigating
failed card tricks and punching my nerve.
Behind the backstop the silver leaf oak and bunch
grass sing softly of a pretension free life, naked
and exuberant. Arms outstretched, momentarily
forgetting my trained embarrassment, I turn home.
Slipping under the covers, warm beside you, I
absorb your love, calm my breath until morning.

Tribute to a Suicide

Breath ends.
Swallowing water
stops
slowly gasping breath,
racing thoughts.

If we pause
we feel pain.
Diving in,
pleasure.
Is there more?

We search
for comfortable boundaries.
When dusk descends,
have we plunged
too far?

What were we to do?
Not sleep and be exhausted at dawn?

Boiling water melts
the cold that floats
us away.

We live
in the world
between
bright lines.

Breath ends.
The rest remain
to find ourselves
in fragile
contentment.

Sheila

A phone call.
The message certain
and irrevocable,
then memory.

Imagine 1960.
Twenty years old,
one-hundred ten pounds, all rubbery bone.
The Iron City in the hills already perfect.

Then,
ecstasy, celebration
drinking, smoking, unimaginable joy
until dawn.
Sure, it would change a girl.

Many years
drinking, smoking,
sensations always sought,
now.

Children, husbands, cities,
in no particular order.
Always,
the city at her heart,
easy there
to find adventure.

To serve and smile.
Life takes its toll.
No regrets. That girl,
tough, world wise,
she makes her happiness
even when breath is short,
the coal colored hair dyed like
the riches of the hills she descended from
now drained.

Even to the end, the black diamond
eyes say, "I've been
there, buster, I've seen
grief and I smile.
No whining from you
buddy boy."

So fitting,
with a stroke
the heart,
gone.
Anticipating another 1960,
never feeling more than dizziness,
sitting with friends.
Why not peace?
That magic moment
confetti descending from plate glass.
Never again.

Lost Child, Gambier 1977

The Ohio winter night blew no colder
than the abandoned love of our vacuumed
creation. Fertile and too young by years
for this exuberantly flawed emotion, we drive
silent beside the slow river.

Sliced, cut, stitched and slammed, a child
left at bay with the illusion of red lipped laughter,
domestic stability. Scoped and cleaned with
sterile metal teasing the cruel secrets of cavalier
consequence from the emptiness and tears of
rumors left on this icy road.

She has lost more than one life, remembering
adolescent rejection, drunk and given no choice
but to confirm that her liberty does not congeal or balm.
What forever will defy convention, guarded
against future romance, prepared for passionate
battle. Beside her, I travel alone, changing.
An empty chair.

Brooding on soaring current, frozen eye,
flesh shall never be fun again. Our neighbor
screams medical murder to youths not ready
to admit finality. For me, another child is born,
a second visitor. Leaving home a graduate
from imagination to knowledge
of the sadness of life.

The Last Clubhouse Eulogy

I stare at the roomful of prospective ghosts
trying to dignify mortality. They tribute the likable
unfortunate, renaming her pain with sunshine,
weighting words with ill-grown dream logic's
weedy asylum. The husband remembers his insoluble
adultery, while the daughter confronts the physical vacuum
of near orphanhood. Ignoring language's inadequacy
they gather collective memories, creating an oracular
familiarity of she recently passed. By a shrewd
pruning of her rueful behavior that does not
convey the obsession of her interior motion, the new
history makes a long and curious morning of beguiling
minimalism. This was no blood blunder. We comfort
only the living. She deafly receives our kind words now.

Border Cemetery

The flower covered broken sidewalk
greets me at the border cemetery.
We are each a territory of one.

The slow memories
of place and mood
dissolve the masks of
gathered family.

Chanting ritual to wake us,
we wait the coming conversations.
They spiral and pierce us.

The chosen one, heavily perfumed, taciturn
leads us to the backyard of her youth,
banishes the contempt between
the loving families
that lie here.

The living continue the myth of their blood, surrender
to a world passed by interstates, malls, and a political
geography more definitive than any reservation, any ocean.

Drowsily, we listen to the witness in the night,
wishing again to dance with a childhood friend,
plump cheeked, curly haired, telling simple narratives,
her only inheritance wrapped in hand me down languor.

She was loved in the fashion of modern office masculinity,
marked by the savvy sleights of counted silence,
beginning a repeated spiritual destruction, welcomed
to the empty banquet with pre-ordained eloquence.

She can not leave this smooth antique neighborhood
of the dead. She stares at the overgrown garden when the
guests have gone, knowing she will be buried, with family,
alone, battered, for having kept this barren lookout.

Diego

No words describe what the senses are given.
The rose sunset bathes the granite range,
the new moon at daybreak challenges the city
lights to surrender their watch. My small universe
wants hope bathed in a morning chill.

The red oak door locks out the danger of the street,
assures I will never know the enchantment encased
behind its white stucco wall. I have imagined children
playing on the sidewalk, curly haired, like mine,
now grown, whose youth is nowhere to be seen.
I circle the city block and delay arrival
at another burdened, routine day.

It is only right that we walk like the old
married couple we pretend to never be,
to an avenue lined with police, in dress black,
filling the cathedral that time does not change,
from ring boy to middle aged mourner.

Diego wears my Tom Thumb silks, lost
in a flurry of tears for grandfather gone
too young, oblivious to the coffin's tale
and what these pews say. It is his
child's smile, surrounded by family
I take with me, glowing,
into the winter sun.

Not Finding the Artist's Grave

5:33 a.m. My new life starts.
I listen to unknown poets,
visitors with truths
who redeem us from the world,
taking ordinary words from darkness,
from memory.

At dawn I see the idle hundreds
mourn the innocent. I cry
for the tortured soul who maimed them,
creating saints without prayers, reward
enough to maim again.

There is nothing extraordinary on this first
day of difference, a step towards discarding
a world that suffocates and trivializes. Finding
mentors, forgetting birthdays of blood, remembered
with blood, available on any calendar to mark and
ignore love and lies and all we have of time.

If something happened up the road, where poets
visited and mourned, something special between
the one you admire and the one you might have known
by one degree of separation, then the new life
commands: travel that road, find that place.
It will not be the same, elusive in time.

Instead I sit, afraid to feel the void of what is there.
Maybe this time, shedding the old
skin, mystery will reveal itself. No,
I will not change. Stare at the dead tree
that stands rotten, not taken
by progress, fashion or authority.
It needs no map to find its place.

The road to salvation is where we remain,
in a lifetime of surprise, delighted
at our daily reception.

Pointless Young Motorcycle Death

Approaching the open
casket
vacancy filled.

Rawboned garages
silent
unhinged
by light and dust.

The greeter claws
at notoriety,
failing to describe
the unpredictable flight to darkness.
Beauty lost in smoking truth,
a half-witted beery glory
bemused.

Left to stare at an odious decline
the surging engine rolls over
the swollen tattooed belly
scorned in private memory.
Time is an ugly fable
unsuitable for misery or respect.

Tired blondes geared in simplicity
round the wooden trunk,
expressions suspended in front row
piety. Bad fashion mirrors the drunken
grace, ships the knotty box to vacancy,
pleasing cold hearts left unloved.

The young deserve a view, too,
at the brief end,
plunged into
spiritual poverty, finished.

Cop Kills Lover, Turns Gun on Self

Mistrusted laughter sprawls
into a bedroom of silence.
The detached tribe of power
echoes the dangerous.
Mistakes tangle with melancholy.

Dark work embraces shadows,
and vanishes alongside the
woman's cherished promise
that would not return
desire.

The empty heart berates deception.
Blurred at the root, there is no joy
in ordinary mending.
Jerked eruptions erase the good,
empty bowels bleed into the ground.

Dancing with himself
the shooter turns a bleak
stone tumor inward.
His roused unraveling exposes
false brilliance.

A single insular rhythm
natural in its shame leaves one
clue. An empty shell for the lover
left behind, praying for eternity.

Japanese Death Poem

Dull is death's anticipation,
there being no easy way
out of this world.
We spend our last days
numbing our nerve against
our journey to the worms.
All lives end resenting what
is forever lost — this earth,
this firm foundation.

Other Books from Chax Press

And many more. Please visit http://chax.org for more information.